A Grain of Sand

A grain of Sand

Poem by P.K. Page
Illustrated by Vladyana Krykorka

Fitzhenry & Whiteside

Published in Canada by Fitzhenry & Whiteside, 195 Allstate Parkway, Markham, Ontario L3R 4T8
Published in the United States by Fitzhenry & Whiteside, 121 Harvard Ave., Suite 2, Allston, Mass. 02134

www.fitzhenry.ca   godwit@fitzhenry.ca

10 9 8 7 6 5 4 3 2 1

National Library of Canada Cataloguing in Publication

Page, P. K. (Patricia Kathleen), 1916-
A grain of sand / P.K. Page ; illustrated by Vladyana L. Krykorka.

ISBN 1-55041-801-7 (bound)

I. Krykorka, Vladyana II. Title.

PS8531.A34G73 2003   jC811'.54   C2002-905765-5
PZ7

U.S. Publisher Cataloging-in-Publication Data (Library of Congress Standards)

Page, P.K. (Patricia Kathleen), 1916-
A grain of sand / P.K. Page ; illustrated by Vladyana L. Krykorka. – 1st ed.
[28] p. : col. ill. ; cm.

Summary: Through poetry and art, the author and illustrator enter the magical mystical world of a child's
imagination. Originally written for an oratorio by composer Derek Holman and first performed in Toronto in
celebration of the millennium.

ISBN 1-55041-801-7

1. Canadian poetry — 20th century. I. Page, P.K. II. Krykorka, Vladyana L. III. Title.
811.54 21 PR9199.3.P354. 2003

Fitzhenry & Whiteside acknowledges with thanks the Canada Council for the Arts, the Government of Canada
through the Book Publishing Industry Development Program (BPIDP), and the Ontario Arts Council for their
support for our publishing program.

Printed in Hong Kong

Design by Blair Kerrigan/Glyphics

For my granddaughter, Anne,
who thought it should be a book,
and for her beautiful children
to whom she will read it.

P.K.P.

To Jack, with all of my love.

V.K.

To see a World in a Grain of Sand,
And a Heaven in a Wild Flower,
Hold Infinity in the palm of your hand,
And Eternity in an hour.

William Blake

Only a fly with its compound eye
Or an ant, a beetle, a dragonfly,

Or a child on a beach on a summer day
With time to idle the hours away,

In the tiniest grain of sand can see
A limitless world of mystery,

With suns that circle and stars that shoot
And golden boughs bearing silver fruit,

Can see in a daisy in the grass
Angels and archangels pass,

Unfolding wings of dazzling white
To set the darkening earth alight.

See outer space become so small
That the hand of a child could hold it all.

Know eons pass, an hour slip by,
like a scudding cloud in a windy sky.

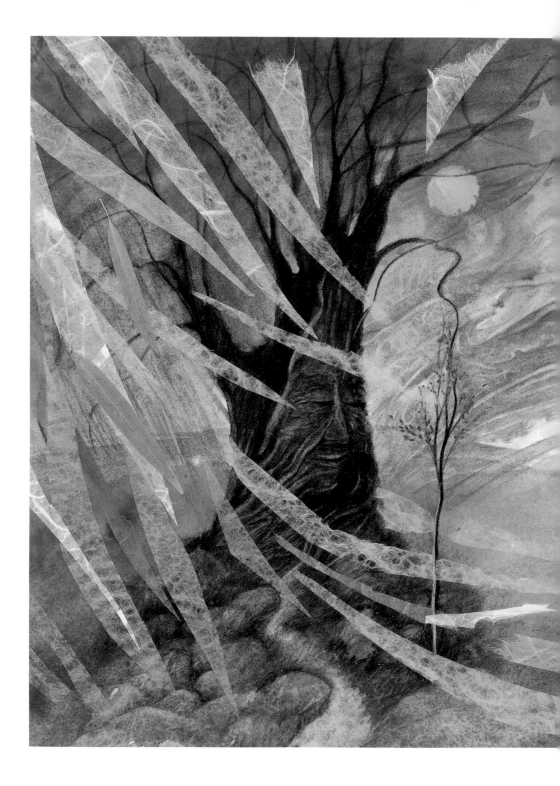

With a wink or a blink an Age is done.
Old Father Time is a boy again.

To see a World in a Grain of Sand,
And a Heaven in a Wild Flower,
Hold Infinity in the palm of your hand,
And Eternity in an hour.

William Blake

A Grain of Sand was written at the request of Derek Holman for his oratorio, An Invisible Reality. Commissioned by Nicholas Goldschmidt, it was performed in June, 2000 at Roy Thomson Hall, Toronto, by the Toronto Children's Chorus, the Toronto Mendelssohn Choir, and the Toronto Symphony Orchestra under the direction of Jukka-Pekka Saraste.

P. K. Page is one of Canada's best-known and honored poets. Born in England, she was educated in England, Calgary and Winnipeg. She also went on to study art in Brazil and New York. Under her married name P. K. Irwin, she gained a reputation for her drawings and paintings, which have been shown widely. Her many books of poetry have received a number of awards including the Governor General's Award for Poetry and the Oscar Blumenthal Award for Poetry. She is also the author of three acclaimed books for children: *The Travelling Musicians of Bremen*, *A Flask of Sea Water*, and *The Goat that Flew*. Patricia Kathleen is a Life Member of the League of Canadian Poets and an Officer of the Order of Canada. She now lives and writes in Victoria, British Columbia.

Vladyana Krykorka was born and raised in Prague, Czech Republic. An only child who loved art, she attended an art high school before going on to study Architecture at the University of Prague. After moving to Canada, she attended the Ontario College of Art. Following a career as Art Director for a business publication, Vladyana began illustrating textbooks, which led her to picture books. She has illustrated over twenty outstanding titles for children, including *Northern Lights – The Soccer Trails*, which won the Ruth Schwartz Award and was listed on the Aesop Accolade list. In addition, she was a silver medal winner of the Mr. Christie Book Award for both *Twelve Months* and *The Polar Bear's Gift*. An artist versatile in many mediums, Vladyana works in her home studio in Toronto, Ontario, where she creates anything from clothing to greeting cards.